BIRTHRIGHT

BIRTHRIGHT

Boudicca Eades

Copyright © Boudicca Eades, 2021

All rights reserved. No part of this book may be reproduced or used in any manner without written permission of the copyright owner except for the use of quotations in a book review.

Cover image by Naomi Ibbotson.

–for Emm

Contents

Sally 3

Summer

Holiday 6

The Beach 8

Words With Grandparents 10

Her Girl 12

Mercy 16

Sweet-talk 18

Trials 22

Clover 24

Autumn

Lycoris Radiata - Hell Flower 30

Lifeline 32

Ever After 34

Teenage Love Poem 36

Wonderland 40

The Poet Says 42

Prolonging The Meal 44

Birthright 46

Winter

Snowfall 52

Broken 54

Lover 56

Music Therapy 58

Gifted 60

My Island 62

Disaster 64

Arsonist 66

Spring

Alice 70

Peppermint 72

Handle 74

For I Love You 76

Grown Up 78

That Loveliest Garden 80

Landed 84

Steam-clean 86

Sally

I pull myself apart
and stitch the pieces
back together again
so often
I fear
that one day
I will fall from the tower again
ready to sew my heart
back together
and find
I have run out of thread.

Holiday

My sister plucked two bright round oranges
from the little tree
next to the adults' table
as if they couldn't see
and hid them beneath her towel.
The peel pressed against her naked body
fresh from the pool.

She ran to me,
and unveiled the bounty; we ate
like kings that night.

The Beach

The first time we went home together
I sat in the front
leaving you stranded in a strange car,
pebbles in your shoes.
You didn't quite know
where to put your hands

so I looked at you
over the shoulder of my seat–
I thought it was a metaphor for us.

The second time we went home together
we sat in the back,
my sister between us,
salt water in her hair,
embarrassing stories on the tip
of her tongue.

We looked at each other
over her shoulders–
I thought it was a metaphor for us.

I thought the ocean
was a metaphor
for you

how I wanted to keep swimming
even as you were pushing me away,
and pulling me closer.

I thought the sun
was a metaphor
for me

but no matter how warm I was
I couldn't quite melt
your clouds.

The third time it was just me
sitting in the back,
driving away from the beach

I *searched*
over the shoulder of my seat.

It was a metaphor for us.

Words With Grandparents

Sitting here, opposite you
in the room with the grey walls
I wonder.

What made your image
of a perfect girl
shatter.

The girl who talked about boys
on the beach with friends
even though she wanted to talk
about girls.
You've been with *that* girl
this whole time.

And I wonder
what has changed
by those three words?

I am
different.

Her Girl

She tells me
that I am
not trustworthy anymore

so it feels like this is the end.

And all I want to do
is drown myself in tea

because somehow
this friendship-lost
feels like that time,
before I was better.

But I'm not losing myself
now.

And everyone says
"she'll come round"
and I know she won't

because she's so proud
and when you're *her girl*
eventually
you'll be the one crawling back,

no matter how many times
you swear
she'll be the one to apologise,

because somehow
this friendship-lost
feels like rain,
and sleepless nights

or drowning
without someone
to throw down the ring.

I almost can't stand
this *thing*
between us

so I'll sit
waiting and
waiting and
waiting

until I give in.

'Cause I'm *her girl* always have been.

Mercy
in response to the story of Mercy Brown

There is something
symbolic
in the story
of a girl
called Mercy

whose heart was
burnt
to crisp, black
snowflakes

and crushed
under her brother's boots–
red, and aching, and young
in her grave.

And for a moment
even her ashes were beautiful.

But the men of the of the village
made mud of them,
and drank
to the vampire
that was never
inside her.

For in death
her body
wields so much power
that it has to be consumed
by them.

Sweet-talk

Before the pandemic we were
an ecosystem thriving off each other,
losses and gains.

We made lines across from mirrors
like workers on pay day
or girls at a sample sale,

trying to find the best deal:
"My nose is too pointy
but at least I like my cheekbones.",

"How are you so beautiful?"
we'd both say.

Buy one get one free on self-loathing
today,
and tomorrow.

Loving each-other's
reflections
in that ever-flowing river,
the drug of fitting in.

Now it's just lonely.

We missed bluebell season
so none of them were trod on,

not a single bright blossom,
not a single girl.

Staring at the glass.

If only you were here in person
to continue the tradition
of mirror-facing conversation.

"Do you think we'll ever be happy?"

you'd ask holding the eyelash curler
to your perfect eyelashes,

"…Have I even made a difference?"

I wouldn't know if you're talking about the curler
or something greater,

"Of course"

I'd say.
We all make a difference, in our own little way,
even now

we're not supposed to admit
we want to talk to someone.
Whilst we're apart
the river has run dry,

everyone only a click away
it feels wrong.

There's a kind of don't care, go-with-the-flow,
you-mean-nothing-to-me attitude
we've grown used to.

Now, in isolation, left with my own thoughts
and body and life to comment on

there is no unspoken deal
I raise you up, you raise me up.

There is no sweet-talking with flesh.

Trials

They will tell you
you are guilty.
They will hunt you down,

they will drag you
through the streets
for the commoners to laugh at.

They are scared
of what
you
can do.

The noose will already be
around your neck
before
the trial
has
begun.

The noose was around
your neck
from the moment
you were
born
this way.

But don't worry.

The judge swings a gavel
of broken reason
and calls it justice.

The witness speaks
in prejudice
and calls it truth.

They
still think you are guilty.
They
won't know better,

but
sitting in the gallery
are the people
who will save you,
and we know

you have not lied.

The only thing you are guilty of
is being you.

Clover

The sun beat down hot those days,
evening turned to night
and still the light

remained in the sky.
Cold sweat clung to the back of my neck,
short hair grown out

from what was once a
buzzcut. By all accounts
I *felt*,

broken, maybe fierce–
fingers closed tightly
around sharp shards of metal:

knives letting loose
at the target,
a field of clovers at my feet.

Sunburn blossoming on
my shoulders,
that summer was hot.

Hotter than any
I had remembered
before,

skin sticky,
mind foggy,
endless exhaustion

somehow made
you feel
alive

yet hazy.
In all the chaos
of midsummer madness

every day was different.
We sat in our girl groups
like a pack of wolves

mouths watering at the smell of gossip,
ready to strike anybody who dared
take more than their share.

It was the season of heartbreak,
of snapping jaws
and fingers on stomachs

and words that bit more than they should.
But it was also the season of forgiveness
and learning

that if I couldn't be one of the boys
in all of their loud glory
at least I could be one of the girls,

still lost in the woods
silent but deadly
fighting to survive

with all of our passion
looking for the four-leaved clover.

Lycoris Radiata - Hell Flower

I climbed the hill to see the flowers
but now they are crushed,
like broken bodies
beneath my heels.

Everything I touch seems to die.
Smash on the ground
after leaping out of my hand,
or my heart.

Out! Damned spot!

The mantra in my head
as I try to erase the past.
Out of guilt.
Out of fear.

Lifeline

You are a crackling
on the dead end
of a telephone line,

the push and release
of buttons stuck by age,

a series of beeps
an automated voicemail
message,

and then silence:
a system failure.

Ever After

Poetry is my medication.
I hold the
pristine pages
to my chest,
cling to each word
as if it is a
lifeline,
wish
I could be sucked into the
sentences,
days in loop.
Trapped in a castle
somewhere
no one can find me.
A fairytale on
repeat
where the princess
is never rescued
but at least there
is quiet.

Teenage Love Poem

we revel in being different,
but doesn't that make us the same?
                                                          we live
we love holding our breath;
it doesn't mean we can breathe under water.

                                         barely afloat

we adore people who get our hopes up,
hate it when they let us down,
                                                down
still hold on to the times they didn't.
stay up late at night
                                         on our luck
wondering if its feminist
to want to be wanted.
                                             wanting

decide that it isn't,
decide that it was probably the shade of lipstick

                                     something different

or the shape of your nose
that made him give up.
                                             to give up

so we set up camp,
and watch rom-coms till our eyes bleed.

                                        on waiting

and sometimes
it's easy.

                                        and hoping

because sometimes
it's better to live

                                        and trying

and hope
it was all a bad dream.

                                      is everything

we live for the makeup moments,
the ones with fingers in hair,

                                        set in stone

dancing to trashy pop music,
it's ok because you're getting over something.

                                        we need

and everyone admits it's a "bad song"
but still we keep listening.

                                        action

for those scarce seconds,
no one judges.

                                        nothing else

and the next morning we wake up
feeling like idiots
                                                              to say
but
the next morning we wake.
                                                              wake up
sleep deprived
and broken;
                                                    break this cycle
maybe in another life
–or the future– still awake
                                                       we are still
for the sounds of birds
that are not extinct.
                                                        holding on
for the voices of people
who are not dead,
                                                        to a world
treading along the beach of a seaside town
that is not destroyed.
                                         without consequences
months later maybe
we have an epiphany,
                                                             this

it creeps in our ears like a bug
whispering beautiful things,

                              is our inheritance

that version of the world:
so much time we could dedicate to surviving

                                    forever
but we don't have to try anymore.

                                    forever

Wonderland

They say she wasn't all quite there
in the head.

I mean
teachers said
that her attitude
to aptitude
lacked.

School reported
"Could do better, she's always off in *wherever*".

Still a
bright girl
heart of gold,
never even got a cold
wouldn't miss a day of school
no interest in being cool.

Shrunk back
into her disappearing act–
she'd learnt from the best.

Ultimate death of the author:
a father who left his daughter
to fend
for herself, to find a way,
pushed towards a getaway.

"Girls should be silent
never heard."

But when she speaks
it's not the absurd
she was told to hear

in her own voice.
No more falling on deaf ears.

Despite everything
she rose above
all the shame

and swore not to treat her daughters
the same.

The Poet Says

Between sets
the poet says
that someday soon
she might have to ruin her life
and then you'll get another book.

I watch her pink-powdered lips
say the words.
It's a joke
but no one laughs.

Isn't this what we came for?
To sit in this crowded room
and listen
to her life

catching glimpses of our own
as her verse bounces off the sticky floor.
From down here
she seems perfect:

someone who's got through it
and she's teaching us
to do the same.

Still we teeter with her, on the edge
of letting the life-ruiner
out.

We are bound to our shadow-selves

Prolonging The Meal

The table is set with invisible plates
and knives
and forks.

We are prolonging the meal
but there's nothing
on the table.

We are wasting time,
until the day we hit eighteen
that's when our life begins
and ends

and I know we won't be friends
when we are thirty
–if there's still a world.
It's unsustainable.

So you don't have to talk to me
and I don't have to interest you

because we are just teenagers
behaving like children

drawing patterns on the table
with water,
an invisible, floral
table runner,

playing grown ups.

Birthright

I watch you retreat
umbrella in hand,
swagger in your step,
and I am alone
and cold
and waiting
–without your umbrella–
for a bus.

In this yellow light,
beneath a dripping streetlamp,
I am suddenly aware of my body
and the way my mother warned me
of the dangers darkness brings.

"Don't stay out too late."
"Remember every licence plate."
Not even this well-worn armour
passed down from mother to daughter
is enough
to keep me from envisioning
each nightmarish scene

inherited through my grandmother's blood–
the generations who sat and listened
to all the ways in which
we could end up dead in a ditch.

Mouth full of dirt,
no more skirts to wear
or calls to be made,
lost knowledge:
how to turn key to blade.
All those wasted cans of pepper spray
littering the path to our graves.

Spatters of drug-detecting nail-polish,
precaution, innovation
not even purity
can be our salvation.

Immeasurable is the fear
of what is lurking in the shadows,
knowing
that a streetlamp
and a camera
cannot save us.

Fight or flight–
the moment the bus arrives
I hold my breath;
what fresh horrors wait inside?
Nothing but a group of drunk boys
who do not hurt me
this time.

Still the journey is haunted
by echoing wolf-whistles
and unwanted touches.

Is all this terror not the same
as the pain we're avoiding?
All the hearts
that need patching?
Every night
spent holding on
to this birthright?

Snowfall

Has the white shroud
settled
around our house
this year?

Frosted flowers
echo
the icy conversation inside.

We pile blankets
over our valuables.
We're all so full
of warming brandy.

I'll want so much to forgive,
once you go back
to your sun-soaked winter.

Broken

You were the first to see me cry.

I came to you
shielding myself from the waves,
seeking refuge;

you were my rock
in a turbulent time.

When I looked again you were
water
trickling away;
I was barely able
to catch you.

You listened with one ear,
the other trained to the ocean;

you said I was broken.
Maybe I am broken.

But you treated broken
like a beautiful piece of glass,
like china.
Then things turned sour–

holding my hand
from a distance,

tip-toeing around,
watching me fall
before even trying to catch me,

pretending to care
just so you can play the hero.

Lover

It seems the boy walks in
nonchalantly eating an apple

in every romance
I have ever read.

He looks at us,   (the girls)
where we are   (where they are)
at a table,   (in love)
penniless, starving,

and takes a bite.

Bad-boy-gone-good,
goes bad again,

the not-quite-dream-girl,
still dreams
of fixing him.

'Cause once upon a time
he would have sacrificed
everything
for her
pure body.

Rip off her clothes
and she's just like any other girl
in this story:

another half-written
character,
bending to his will.

Music Therapy

I hold you
in my head
like a tune
I can't quite
remember.
But play it
over and
over and
over
again,
as if
a musical shadow
is enough
to keep me from
slipping
into a pattern
of
overthought apologies
and hour long
arguments
in my head,
replacing them
with the drone
of someone else's voice.

Is that what they mean
by Music Therapy?
Blaring the sound
into your ears
until it goes straight
into your
head?
Forcing your heart
to either
wallow
in its own or another's
pain?
Sound seeps
into your soul,
rumbles
and cries
of things worse
than anything
you could think of.
A crack
of thunder,
for the oncoming
rainstorm.

Gifted

She is the creator
of her own
world.

Words fold themselves
over her lips–
loud, brash origami,

knotted, garbled, twisted over
one another.
Unraveling

chaos leaping through our ears
sacred only
to her.

And oh the dead
she could wake,
loud and booming,

startled from their sleep–
a library of fools.
Chanting

*Be quiet.
We don't want your
persistent, forked tongue.*

Not in our holy heads.

My Island

I am scared of the thin layer
of fat
surrounding my ribs.
The way I can pull it away from the bone
seems like too much, an excess.
It is there to keep me warm
but maybe if I can be cold enough,
shiver enough,
burn enough calories,
it would drop off

gone.
Like the time I could have spent living,
gone.
Like the year I thought I hadn't wasted
only to find myself
here,
back at the beginning.

Last Christmas I drowned myself in
homemade fit-tea
and an invisible diet.
The science said it would take three weeks
of not eating
before I started to starve
but maybe if I could be empty enough,
drink enough,
I would be slim enough for school.

And now instead
of writing New Year's resolutions
I find myself penning
a list of fears and problems
in the hope
that next year
I will finally be out of the woods
and off this damn island.

Disaster

When a lightning bolt
strikes nearby
you're supposed to
stop drop and roll.

The pamphlet says
the only thing
you can do
is hope
you don't get hit.

And when the air
around you fries,
it's too late.

What the leaflet couldn't tell me
was how to deal
with speechlessness.

How to get by
with no breath,
with the residue left

from feeling
so sheer and defenceless?
You could
hold me up to the window

and the room would still
be lit the same.

Because how could
I be more
than a pair
of useless
lace curtains?

Imobile, and invisible
as I feel,
wishing

that lightning
would strike me where I stand.

Arsonist

Smoke screen
seen from space

screams and shouts
seem to replace

the status quo:

a dozen refugees
floating away from the burning trees.

In this age of deniers
it is difficult to relate the public to the private,
ignorance to flame

put your feet up, everything will stay the same.

A whole nation is burning
and we keep turning
the page to a new story–

one that will "delight" us more than the last
but maybe you just can't be arsed.

There is comfort
in thinking you could not do anything
to stop it,

that God
or spirits
or arsonists

are responsible
for setting forests aflame

–still the weather just doesn't feel the same–

that every time
you turn a blind eye
look at the facts
and still ask why,

every comment you send,
every false conspiracy you think
brings

doubt–
something you can't live without.

Alice

A relic of childhood past
sits on my shelf,
painted eyes staring at me
through a plastic fringe.

The crack in her cheek
tells of years
playing,
being played with.

Propped up at tea parties,
forced to speak
through that half-open mouth,
eternally agape.

Two generations
of fingerprints
have left their mark,
two unfinished souls.

Fragile,
full of cracks
and darkness
inside.

Now dust
litters her hair.
Illuminated by the golden sun,
she has been left alone.

I will take care of you
darling, darling dolly.

Peppermint

There is something
so wonderful
about
peppermint tea.

Too many times
I have drowned
myself
in its strange ability

to cleanse and
to warm
my soul.

Its comforting
aroma
makes it easier
to breathe.

Handle

I used to think
my hands were big enough

to hold
both of our pain,

to stoke
both of our fires,

to ward off
both our demons,

but every time
I tried to grasp
your cup in my hand
my cup went cold.

I realised I couldn't even start
to think about
helping you
when I hadn't cured myself.

And although my hands
may not yet
be big enough

to hold
both of our pain,
to stoke
both of our fires,
to ward off
both our demons,

I can put a kettle
on the stove for you;

I can tend to the flames
whilst watching the water boil

and make tea for both of us.

For I Love You

To my father / who has had books on parenting and self-esteem and mindfulness and stoicism / piled on his desk for as long as I can remember / my routine is not foreign– / all the winter rush / summer sadness / familiar and dreaded– / like most bad habits only works / the first hundred times. / And to my mother / who painted patches / of different whites / all around our house and / never chose / a single one / before we moved out; / she understands / depression / the sadness that can creep in / through the open window / or change with the wind / and my sister, / so excited we all call her a / sugar addict / but have her in the house / 'cause sugar doesn't perish / we can all use a little sweetness sometimes right? / And it doesn't matter if we dip or cry / this is our little family / no matter what.

Grown Up

My sister followed
in my footsteps
like a shadow,
but kinder.

She learnt
to call
every boy I let
into our home
"brother".

Every boy she
brought into our home
"boyfriend", "partner",
"lover",

although
the words hadn't yet
acquired meaning.

Naming
each love letter I wrote
a *mistake*,

every mistake I made
a love letter
to myself.

That Loveliest Garden

The grass is always greener
on the other side.
So we shrank.
Until we were small enough
to fit
into *their* big, wide, world.

Fountains
and rose bushes
and paper men
waiting for us:
girls who would give them life,
one day maybe a wife,

we tried so hard.
Always too big for the house,
too small for the garden,
years of hips on doorknobs
and tripping over stairs
we wanted to be *theirs*,

we wanted to explore.
Reach in,
fall in,
take everything
at face value.
We have to fit.

All the pain,
like smoke billowing
from a chimney,
has no place
in that loveliest garden.
What will we find?

We swam through
our own oceans;
millions of teardrops.
We got smaller and smaller,
but it turns out
we don't need to shrink

to nothing,
to see their world
as it is:
a little less wondrous,
a little less beautiful.

Puddles and
thorns and
playing-card boys.

Landed

I stick my muddied fingers
into the mossy bank,
toes dangling,
bribing the river with my sweetness.

I am queen of the forest–
a wild kingdom towering with trees,
peaceful and solid
and everything I'm not.

'Though its earth is swollen
with salt and raindrops
we always remember
the summer hot.

Steam-clean

The steam rising
out of my cup
encourage

the tears
prickling
in my eyes...

Have they come
to say
farewell?

I look to a time when
this is behind me,
water under the bridge.

Kelp-covered toes
firmly on the shore,
a mis-placed doll
dirtied by soil and water,
torn apart,
put back together.
Steam-cleaned
'till only the stubbornest stains
remain.

Found again,
I will deliver myself
in my own fragile-taped
box

back home.

Notes

P.16

Mercy is inspired by the story of Mercy Brown, one of the best documented cases of the exhumation of a corpse to banish the undead. She was just one victim of the New England vampire panic.

P.30

Lycoris Radiata - Hell Flower is named after the red spider lily, a flower associated with goodbyes and said to guide people through the cycle of rebirth.

P.66

Arsonist includes text taken from and inspired by the news coverage surrounding the Australian bushfires in 2019-2020.

P.40 & P.80

Wonderland and *That Loveliest Garden* are both inspired by the work of Lewis Carroll

Acknowledgements

Thank you to the Poetry Foundation for my commendation in the *Foyle Young Poets of the Year Award 2021* and for first publishing *Holiday* online in their winner's anthology.

With thanks to my parents, for all your love and support in this project. You have always encouraged me to follow my passions and for that I will forever be grateful.

Thank you to my sibling, whose excitement has spurred me on.

To my friends who read earlier drafts of this book and helped it become what it is now: Remy Duke, Eva Correard, and Sofia Tagliani Beltran. Without you this book would not have come nearly as far.

With thanks to my teachers, who too read earlier drafts of this book and never doubted me.

Finally with thanks to my mentor and editor Eva Hibbs, for your unerring support and honesty, for the time you spent working through these poems. This collection would not be possible without you.

Printed in Great Britain
by Amazon